Makers of African

GW00392261

Shaka, King of the Zulu
The herd-boy who founded a nation

Richard Woolley

Longman

Longman Group Limited
London

*Associated companies, branches and representatives
in Africa and throughout the world*

© Longman Group Ltd 1973

First published 1973
Third impression 1978

ISBN 0 582 60264 5

Printed in Hong Kong by Wah Cheong Printing Press Ltd.

Contents

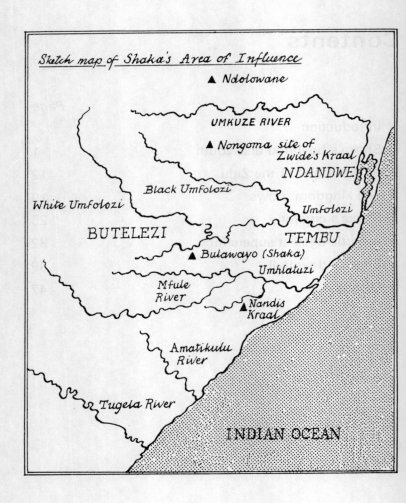

Sketch map of Shaka's Area of Influence

▲ Ndolowane

UMKUZE RIVER

▲ Nongoma site of Zwide's Kraal

NDANDWE

Black Umfolozi

White Umfolozi

Umfolozi

BUTELEZI

TEMBU

▲ Bulawayo (Shaka)

Umhlatuzi

Mfule River

▲ Nandis Kraal

Amatikulu River

Tugela River

INDIAN OCEAN

Introduction

This is the story of the founder of a nation—Shaka, king of the Zulu.

Shaka built up his armed forces from small beginnings, for he started with less than five hundred men in a tiny territory of little more than a hundred square miles. Eventually, he commanded the largest army ever raised in Africa; a force trained under his direction in the use of shield and stabbing spear and made up of highly skilled warriors drawn from many different tribes over a vast area, which he united into one great people, the Zulu, which in their language means *Heaven*.

Shaka liked to think of himself as the bravest of all chiefs, but he was also said to be the most cruel, for dreadful stories are told of the deaths he inflicted upon his own and other people; with him death was swift and merciless.

Tales are told of his fearlessness; of how he killed wild animals unaided, of his deeds as a soldier and of how he fought against the superstitions taught to the people by the witch-doctors.

Shaka was born in shame, for he was the illegitimate son of Senzangakona, then a very minor chief of a minor tribe, the Zulu, but it seems that shame made him struggle the harder to succeed.

He became famous and performed many memorable

deeds in a very short time, for he was king of the Zulu for twelve years only. Then he was killed by his brothers, who tried to destroy everything he had built up. In a short while all Shaka's work was undone.

Chapter 1
Shaka's boyhood and youth

Shaka was born in 1787 into a land now known as
Natal in the Republic of South Africa, which was then
a land free and open to all; to those born there, to
those who lived there and to those who were to come
there to make their homes. It was a land free for men
to hunt or to cultivate as they wished and where a man
decided where he would build his first hut and eventually raise his family in his own kraal. Although the
word 'kraal' is used to describe a number of huts
gathered together inside a fence, it is also used to
describe the homestead and the family unit, many of
which made up a clan.

He was born unwanted and illegitimate. When his
mother, Nandi, was found to be pregnant, her family
sent a message to the elders of the clan Zulu, to which
her lover, Senzangakona, belonged. The elders would
not believe Nandi's family.

They sent back a message, 'The girl has a beetle
(*Shaka*) in her belly'.

However, Nandi did become a mother and she and
her son were sent to the Zulu clan with a further
message, 'Here is the *Shaka*'.

Love between Nandi and Senzangakona had ceased,
and without ceremony she was taken into the kraal and
given the status of third wife. The baby boy was
called *Shaka* and both he and his mother were neglected
and unhappy, except for a short time after Nandi gave
birth to another child, a daughter called Nomcoba.

While a small boy of six years old, Shaka allowed a dog to kill one of his father's sheep, which made Senzangakona so angry that he chased Nandi and her two children from his kraal. There was nowhere for her to go, and so she was forced to return to her own family.

Shaka hated his mother's people, the Langeni, but always worked hard looking after their herds of cattle and goats. One day his herd was attacked by a black mamba snake. During the struggle a prize black bull was killed, but Shaka, then aged thirteen years, bravely attacked and killed the snake. The Langeni chief called Shaka to his kraal and told him that he had heard of his bravery in killing the snake and gave him a goat as a reward. But this made Shaka no happier, for he suffered the sneers and cruel taunts of the other boys who called him 'fatherless' and he felt unwanted by everybody.

At fifteen years of age Shaka was sent back to his father's kraal for his initiation ceremony. An important part of this ceremony was the presentation from the father to the initiate son of a front-apron, the *umutsha*. Before they were fifteen years old, all boys were completely naked. Shaka refused this present from his father, and he was sent back to his mother.

After many moves from place to place and kraal to kraal with many bitter experiences, including famine, Shaka at last found some security as a herd-boy with a headman called Ngomane of the Mtetwa tribe. Here he was classed as a senior and received the respect of his juniors. It was in these days at the age of sixteen to seventeen that Shaka began to show his powers of leadership. He formed his fellow herd-boys into a gang

2

and taught them how to throw spears and fight with sticks.

At nineteen Shaka killed his first big wild animal, when he tackled the fiercest of all the beasts, the leopard, single-handed with two throwing spears and a club. Though he did not kill it with his first spear, he bravely stood his ground when the infuriated animal attacked him, and killed it with his club and his second spear.

There was great delight in the village and it was decided that Shaka should take the skin to his friend the headman, Ngomane, who would present it to the king of the Mtetwa. Ngomane was so pleased with the event that he gave Shaka a cow, the first one of many thousands which Shaka was eventually to own.

Then something happened which proved very important for Shaka. The chief of Metetwa died and his son, Dingiswayo, took over the tribe and set to work building up an army.

Dingiswayo proved to be a good chief. He had travelled a good deal and had been the guide to a European who had taught him much about the art of warfare and how to handle an army. When the white man was killed by the Quabe, Dingiswayo found himself in possession of a horse and a gun, the most prized belongings of a soldier. He seemed just the kind of man Shaka could follow and admire. Soon Shaka and Dingiswayo became friends.

So, at the age of twenty-one Shaka became a soldier, wearing a uniform of a kilt of fur strips, a skin cap with black feathers, white fringes of ox-tail on his ankles and wrists, and sandals made of hide. He was armed with a shield and three throwing spears or *assegais*.

4

Shaka distinguished himself as a soldier and many times earned the praise of his chief. He told Dingiswayo of how he had thought of a new way of fighting. He explained how it appeared to him that to throw a spear left too much to chance, for one could never be sure whether or not it had found its mark. It was much better to keep the spear and fight with it in the hand.

Dingiswayo watched Shaka in battle catching the spears thrown by the enemy on his shield and then attacking with a stabbing spear against a man who was then unarmed and whose shield Shaka would fling aside by hooking his own underneath. He was proud of such a soldier, but also a little frightened, for he himself was a very kind chief whose desire was not to kill, but to govern well.

Shaka, on the other hand, was always eager to improve as a warrior. He gave up the habit of wearing sandals because he was sure they reduced his speed and he found that his hard tough feet enabled him to overtake a retreating man in sandals.

Certain that he had found a better way of fighting, Shaka also decided that he needed a spear different in design from the one used for throwing, which was not sufficiently strong for close fighting, so he set off to find someone who could make a more suitable weapon.

Away he went in search of a blacksmith who could make what he needed. Blacksmiths were often difficult to find, for they always lived alone in the bush. No one would live near them, because people believed that they forged the best blades with the aid of human fat.

When Shaka arrived at the smith's kraal, people wondered, as they saw him pass, why a man should walk into what they thought was a place of death.

Shaka explained with care just exactly what he wanted.

'Such a blade will cost a lot,' said the smith.

'What will it cost?' enquired Shaka.

'A heifer cannot be too dear for a man like you with this wonderful idea,' answered the blacksmith.

'A heifer it is,' shouted Shaka as he held out his hand to seal the bargain.

Then the blacksmith did something very cruel.

'We need some bellows to blow the fire,' he said. 'We will use the skin of a goat.'

He took five goats, skinned them while they were still alive, and put them in an enclosure to die.

'We will watch them,' said the blacksmith. 'We will use the skin of the one which dies last. That will be the toughest, you may be sure.'

After this horrible event, a new furnace was built and filled with iron and charcoal, and the work of smelting the iron was started. Then it was time to forge the blade for the spear. Then the handle was made by another expert and the blade was fitted into it. Shaka's new spear was ready.

It may be that the blacksmith's cruelty influenced Shaka for the worse in his later life. He was certainly to gain a reputation for cruel deeds. Some people however, say that his experience, and the use of human fat, made him so disgusted that it explains why, later, he was always against magic. As we shall see, when he became king of the Zulu, he discredited the witch-doctors, and put many of them to death.

In great triumph Shaka went back to rejoin his

regiment where everybody was interested in his new weapon.

'Arm all your warriors with this and take away their sandals and we'll conquer Africa,' said Shaka to his chief. 'I will prove it to you, my father Dingiswayo. In our next battle let me call out one of the enemy to single combat and you shall see.'

Dingiswayo was already at war with the Butelezi tribe, and when he called upon their chief to surrender the chief hurled insults at Dingiswayo.

'Send the best man you have in all your tribe and I will have him killed by one of mine.'

'Yes, send him to fight,' shouted Shaka, 'and I tell you, I'll make him eat your words!'

He leapt from the ranks of the men of Dingiswayo's Mtetwa, calling, 'Come and fight! come and fight!'

A flying spear came towards him from the man the enemy chief had sent out to fight. Shaka took it on his shield. As he saw the next one aimed at him Shaka charged with great speed at the Butelezi soldier until he was at close quarters. Then he ripped his enemy's shield away with his own and thrust his new spear right through the man's body.

Dingiswayo's soldiers were so fired with enthusiasm that the battle was the shortest in history. The Butelezi quickly surrendered and acknowledged the Mtetwa chief as their overlord.

One result of this victory was that when Shaka's father, Senzangakona, heard of the defeat of the Butelezi, who were his friends, he volunteered to accept Dingiswayo as his overlord. This, of course, pleased Shaka very much. Moreover, Dingiswayo gave many presents to Shaka, and so did his fellow warriors.

When he came home after the battle he was the owner of about fifty oxen and cows. He was now a rich and important person.

The day after the battle Shaka was called before his chief. Dingiswayo informed him that among the dead of the Butelezi was one of the soldiers of their allies the Zulu. This was a man called Bakuza, who was the son of Senzangakona by another wife and therefore Shaka's half-brother. Shaka had never met this brother and was not at all troubled that he was dead, especially as he did not love his father. Yet he was surprised and very interested when he learned from Dingiswayo that Bakuza had been nominated to succeed as chief of the Zulu on the death of Senzangakona. The news became even more interesting when Dingiswayo asked Shaka if it would please him to replace Bakuza as future chief of the little Zulu tribe.

'That would be my dearest wish, my father-chief,' replied Shaka.

Shaka was full of pride, for now he would soon become chief-designate of the Zulu people. He thanked Dingiswayo, and gratefully began to plan for the future in his mind.

After his long talk with Dingiswayo, Shaka was met by a girl called Pampata. He had only met her once before, but since then they had become attached to each other, and this feeling was to last for the rest of their lives even though they never married.

He was also met by his other love, his mother Nandi, who made arrangements for a great feast for which one of Shaka's prize oxen was slaughtered. Her son's success especially pleased Nandi, who now felt that all her suffering and wanderings had been worthwhile.

Shaka was placed in command of a hundred men and he spent the time training his own little force in the use of the stabbing spear and working out with them just exactly how he would win battles when he became the leader of his own army.

Not very long afterwards, when Shaka was about twenty-four years old, the commander of his regiment, Buze, retired and Shaka took his place, much to the joy of all the soldiers, for they believed in Shaka's ability as a soldier and as a leader.

From that day onwards, as a token or symbol of his command, Shaka always carried a very small specially made red-handled stabbing spear. He was to keep this to the end of his life.

Chapter 2
Shaka: Chief of the Zulu

About this time, Zwide, the chief of a very large tribe, the Ndwandwe, began to cause trouble. He had previously been subdued by Dingiswayo, but he now began to copy Dingiswayo's methods by recruiting a large army.

He was a pitiless and a superstitious man. After a battle, it was his custom to cut off the heads of the enemy leaders and give them to his witch-like mother, Ntombazi, who stored them in her hut.

When he had an army big enough to make war, he attacked a very small tribe led by a most courageous man called Zwangendaba. This man was later to lead his tribe northwards across the great Zambesi river. However, Zwangendaba proved too much for Zwide. Zwide was easily defeated, and, angry at this defeat, he decided he must attempt another campaign. So he enlisted the help of the mighty Dingiswayo in attacking another small tribe. This time he won the battle, but this success made him so arrogant and proud of his victory that Dingiswayo felt he must be taught a lesson.

In order to subdue Zwide, Dingiswayo sent three regiments (totalling less than two thousand men) to take the capital of the country. It was Shaka's plan, and he was so successful that he wiped out about half of Zwide's army.

After the battle, Dingiswayo held a council with all his advisers. 'What should I do with Zwide?' he asked.

'Kill him at once,' said Shaka, 'and kill that terrible old mother of his who collects dead men's skulls. If you don't kill him, he'll kill you and I would not like to think of my father-chief's skull swinging in Ntombazi's hut.'

But Dingiswayo was not a man who believed in killing when the battle was won. Rather, he believed in making friends with his enemies.

He was pressed hard again by Shaka. 'If you let him go, he will kill you. The only safe way with an enemy is to kill him, either in battle or afterwards. I will only treat generously those who submit without a fight, for, although I honour the brave, they must know that they are brave enough to die.'

However, Dingiswayo could not be persuaded to execute his enemy. Instead he fined Zwide a large number of cattle—over two thousand cows and oxen. He was to pay with his life for such mercifulness.

Security was now beginning to come to Shaka. He had many cattle, he felt free and happy. However, even though Nandi, his mother, was anxious that Shaka should marry and kept on reminding him of Pampata and telling him how much she herself longed to become a grandmother, Shaka would not change his mind.

'Take care of Pampata, mother,' said Shaka. 'Keep her always with you, for I shall never marry her, nor shall I marry anyone else.'

Nandi was shocked at this and told Shaka of her grief at his decision, but he was unmoved, for he had definitely decided that marrying was not for him.

Dingiswayo had not forgotten his promise to Shaka about the chieftainship of the Zulu and one day he sent his senior headman, Shaka's friend, Ngomane, to Senzangakona, with a message telling him that Shaka was living under his protection.

Senzangakona was well aware of Shaka's whereabouts and realised at once that such a great man as Dingiswayo, chief of the Mtetwa, wanted him to visit him and at the same time meet his unknown son. Dingiswayo had clearly decided that Shaka should be Senzangakona's heir.

At the festivities held to welcome his guest, Dingiswayo did not introduce Shaka to his father. It was not until Senzangakona enquired about the tall young man, who seemed to be so important and so popular, that he became aware of his own son.

Senzangakona was overjoyed to see what an excellent young man his son had become, and everyone thought, from what he said, that he would nominate Shaka, his eldest surviving son, as his heir. But the promise was not kept, for on his return to his own country, under pressure from one of his wives, Senzangakona appointed a younger son to succeed him. Soon afterwards, Senzangakona died and his burial was marked with all the honours due to a chief, including the burial of personal servants with him. His son, Sigujana, then took over the chieftainship.

When Shaka got to know of this he was very angry and, although he had the power to attack the new chief and crush him, he decided to send his young half-brother to ask Sigujana to give up his position. Unfortunately, however, a fight broke out in which the new chief was killed, and so Shaka was now ready to take over the Zulu. With his own Mtetwa regiment, the Izi-cwe and his old friend and adviser, Ngomane, he set off, dressed in the most glorious attire of blue monkey fur and spotted genet tails.

On arrival at his father's kraal the splendid figure of Shaka brought the people flocking to see him. They were full of admiration and, at Ngomane's request, acclaimed him with great shouts of approval.

Shaka's first task was to build himself an army. First, he found exactly what men he had at his disposal of all age-groups. This was a task something like a modern census when all the people in a country are counted.

After completing his 'census' Shaka split the men into age-groups and then formed them into regiments. The best of these was called the *Fasimba* regiment and was made up of the twenty-year-old youths. These young men had no work to do and Shaka could see they would be pleased to do something brave and productive. Later they became known as 'Shaka's Own Regiment' and with them he built and fortified his kraal. They became his garrison troops and the best of all his great army.

The old blacksmith who had made Shaka's spear *Ixwa* was sent for and set to work to produce stabbing spears in large quantities, though all the ideas of skinning live goats and using human fat for forging were dismissed by Shaka. He said they were wasteful and superstitious and that everyone must concentrate upon the business of manufacturing stabbing spears, rather than on carrying out practices in which he did not believe. This was perhaps the first of his attacks on the old system of witch-doctoring and magic.

Next, he sent a special group of soldiers to fetch his mother in great style and comfort. He put her into the best part of his kraal and gave her the best of attention by the best of all his servants. Later, when he had the time to spare, he made the soldiers build her a kraal of her own.

After he had settled down into his kraal and had everything running the way that he wanted it, Shaka called together his people.

'Here is my mother, Nandi, Ndlovukazi*,' he shouted. 'When she was young she was wronged by our people. She came from the Langeni and was with child —I was that child. Her people sent messages to you and you would not listen. Bring forth my old uncle, Mudli, for he knows all about it. He will tell us about it, my people, in case you have forgotten.'

Mudli, an elder of the tribe and brother of Shaka's father, was brought before the new chief.

'Tell us all the story of the beetle—the story of Shaka—my old uncle. The people would like to hear it,' demanded Shaka.

But Mudli did not speak. He was too frightened.

Shaka's cruel answer to such silence was to have his uncle killed.

From his kraal, which he had called Bulawayo, Shaka now made daily visits to supervise the training of his army, and he was continually demonstrating the art of using the stabbing spear. He had now produced many of these by taking two throwing spears and having them cast into one stabbing spear by the smith.

*'female elephent'

16

He was tireless in his work. Before he could begin to take over other tribes and territories, he had to make sure his men were really well trained and able to fight in the way that he wanted them to do.

To make one great Zulu nation out of all the small warring tribes was Shaka's ambition. He wanted a territory a thousand times bigger than that which the Zulu owned, and he would not be satisfied with anything less than this.

To toughen his men Shaka put them through all kinds of seemingly impossible tasks—those who refused he killed—and the result was an army totally devoted to him and his cause who would risk any danger for the sake of their chief. These were the kind of men Shaka needed if so small a people were to take over tribes a thousand times their number.

As Shaka grew in strength and power so did Pampata. She had long since given up the idea of becoming his wife, but she resolved never to leave him and indeed became one of his best advisers. Shaka in return became as lovingly attached to her as he was to his mother.

At last the new chief was ready to move on to his first conquest, and for this he chose his mother's tribe, the Langeni, who had been so unkind to him and to his mother during the days after they had been made to leave his father's kraal.

All those he could find who had been cruel to either him or his mother he killed. The others he left in peace under their chief, who undertook to acknowledge Shaka as his overlord, for these were his mother's people, and he was content to be assured of their loyalty.

Chapter 3
The kingdom grows

Shaka did not conquer his mother's people with too much cruelty, except for the acts of revenge, and this probably influenced a number of neighbouring tribes to make friendly arrangements with him. So his army grew bigger and bigger and very shortly, with all men trained in the use of the *Ixwa* as their fighting weapon, he had a force of several thousands.

Now his thoughts of further conquest made him turn to the old enemies of Dingiswayo, the Butelezi, who had insulted him and against whom he had first used his stabbing spear with such great success.

The Butelezi did not take Shaka seriously. They thought they would beat him without any trouble and even their women gathered to watch the battle. How wrong they were! Not only did Shaka kill nearly all the soldiers, but he attacked the women and old men as well, and took all the children and all the animals into the Zulu tribe. Only the chief with a few of his men escaped to seek refuge with that other enemy of Dingiswayo, Zwide, chief of the Ndwandwe, and Zwide was soon to become a very troublesome man to Shaka. As before he started to attack many of the neighbouring smaller tribes, some of which he conquered. Feeling full of importance and flushed with success, Zwide turned his attention to Dingiswayo, who had beaten him many times, in order to goad him into yet another war.

Eventually Dingiswayo, after consulting Shaka,

marched with his army to demand of Zwide an end to his seizure of other tribes' land and to make him once more submit to his rule. Dingiswayo had arranged with Shaka for the two to meet near to Zwide's capital, but Dingiswayo arrived first and was invited to talk by Zwide in his kraal.

Foolishly Dingiswayo went into the kraal with only ten of his girls to hold *ndaba* (talk) with Zwide, and under pressure from his evil mother, Ntombazi, Zwide had Dingiswayo murdered at the meeting. So Shaka lost his old friend and protector.

Zwide's army then went out to rout Dingiswayo's forces. Shaka, not knowing what had happened, could only stand and watch, and the Mtetwa forces seemed so shocked by their chief's murder that they were unable to resist the Ndandwe.

Shaka realised that he would be the next to be attacked by Zwide and went home to make intensive preparations. He was resolved he would avenge all that had happened and especially the death of his friend, Dingiswayo. He took into the army men of all kinds, even the old, and began to drill them himself in the use of the stabbing spear. Everyone in Shaka's kingdom responded to the call—the women and children helped with making stocks of food, while the men trained from sun-up to sun-down.

At last Zwide and his Ndwandwe hordes arrived at the river boundary of the land of the Zulu. Shaka was faced with the biggest test of his life. It was April 1818, and Shaka was thirty-one years of age.

Relying on the women and young boys to keep him supplied with food and water Shaka patiently awaited the attack on his own side of the river, knowing that should his opponents cross and leave the river behind them they would soon feel the effect of being without water in that hot month.

On the first day of the attack, Zwide's forces failed to ford the river, so watchful were the Zulu soldiers, who inflicted hundreds of casualties on the Ndwandwe while they were still in the water.

In the evening the river level showed signs of dropping, and this meant that the invaders would soon be able to cross. In the night Shaka thought of something which he felt sure would split the forces of Zwide into two parts. In the morning, in full view of the Ndwandwe, he sent all the cattle, together with some of his troops, towards the far boundary of his land. At the same time he concealed the main part of his army behind a hill. Immediately the Ndwandwe commander detached a large force to go after the cattle, thinking that Shaka was in retreat and was taking his wealth with him to cross the far boundary of his country.

As the detachment of about one-third of Zwide's army gave chase to the cattle, Shaka brought out from behind the hill about fifteen hundred men, leaving some two thousand still in hiding. Seeing this small force confronting them the Ndwandwe, with an army three times the size of Shaka's, charged at the Zulu, hurling their first wave of spears about fifty yards from the Zulu lines. Most of these spears were taken safely on the Zulu shields. In the throwing of their spears the Ndwandwe lines became ragged and out of balance, and the men began to jostle one another. Now many of them could not throw their next wave of spears.

Shaka then ordered his men to charge into this

great horde of screaming soldiers. The Ndwandwe were unable to understand why the Zulu did not return their wave of spears, and were taken by surprise by the stabbing spears. On this first charge the Zulu inflicted dreadful slaughter, and the Ndwandwe retreated to regroup.

Attack after attack took place, always with the same result, until nearly seven thousand Ndwandwe had been killed or wounded.

Near the other border Shaka's men with the cattle had also done well, for although considerably outnumbered they had caused nearly a thousand casualties among their attackers, and though the Ndwandwe captured many of Shaka's cattle in their flight a large number of them were recovered later.

Now Shaka's fame grew throughout the whole of the area. The Mtetwa, who had no chief now that Dingiswayo was dead, eagerly joined forces with their old comrade Shaka and the Zulu. Shaka could now raise an army of about 10,000 men, much stronger than that of any other chief, and he decided that while his lieutenants trained his army he would devote himself to other matters dealing with the welfare of his country. He turned his attention to the improvement of the strain of cattle in his country and introduced new laws which would make sure that a better type of herd was built up.

He even had time to spare for an effort to revive the folk festivals of the Zulu, and at a great gathering of the whole of his people he celebrated the harvest and gave new laws and cancelled others. He was received with acclamation by all his people; and always near were his mother, Nandi, and his love, Pampata.

Shaka always had to live with the knowledge that one day the Ndwandwe would return to attack his country and much of the time while he relaxed was taken up in planning for the future, for that day when the hordes of Ndwandwe would come swarming into his country for the second time.

One asset of the Zulu chief was his efficient intelligence service, for every day he received reports on what was taking place in the land of the Ndwandwe. One day he was informed of an intended invasion which was to take place after the harvest. Zwide intended to kill every person in Zululand and take all their crops to feed his own people. So, when the harvesting of the crops was completed, Shaka ordered that everything should be collected in grass bags and taken into the Nklandla forest where it was to be stored in caves or buried in the earth.

When he found that the Ndwandwe were preparing to march, Shaka moved all his people from his river frontier to the far boundary, thus allowing the enemy a free passage through his territory.

The Ndwandwe were surprised. There was not a Zulu to be seen anywhere—kraals were empty—the cattle had vanished—and the whole country was deserted.

The enemy had set out from their country with bread and meal and a number of cattle to last them for three or four days, believing that they could rob the Zulu of their harvest and so support themselves; but now they found that this was impossible. The Ndwandwe went deeper into Zululand, looking for food until they reached the forest where the grain was stored.

At nightfall Shaka sent several hundred of his men into the forest so that they could attack in the darkness. Many of the Ndwandwe were killed silently in the night, and next morning, hungry, tired and very worried, the demoralised troops were confronted by all the rest of Shaka's fresh, well-fed, well-slept soldiers, who slaughtered the entire force.

This accounted for half of the army sent by Zwide to subdue the Zulu. The other half, having been held in reserve, now tried to cross the river, but Shaka had sent more of his troops to cross by a ford some distance from where the Ndwandwe were gathered, and it was not until the Zulu attacked them from the rear that they were even aware of their existence. They, too, were killed.

Meanwhile, Shaka had already sent a small invading force into Ndwandweland to capture Zwide and his evil mother, Ntombazi. They killed everything in sight, men, women, children, dogs, everything except the cattle; but they were unable to find Zwide, for he had escaped and gone north with the remnants of his tribe. However, Ntombazi was taken captive and held in her hut to await the arrival of Shaka.

Apart from Zwide, only three commanders and a few soldiers escaped. Shaka was now completely safe as overlord of his own and many surrounding countries.

Chapter 4
Shaka's cruelty

Shaka showed great generosity in victory to his own men. Many of the families of Shaka's soldiers who had died were awarded gifts of cattle, as were those who had commanded the victorious troops. But he also revealed something of the cruelty which seemed to grow as his power increased.

He had no reason to show much pity to Ntombazi. She was an evil and cruel woman who had schemed to deceive and to destroy Shaka's friend Dingiswayo.

But Shaka's revenge for Dingiswayo's death, and for Zwide's attack on the Zulus, was horrible indeed. Because Ntombazi claimed that her power came from the hyena, Shaka questioned her on this magic.

'And to you, Ntombazi, the hyena is the sign of witchcraft?'

'Oh, yes,' replied Ntombazi. 'He's much more than that. He's the animal I hold in my spell. He's the animal on whose back I ride. He's the animal I possess and over which I have absolute power.'

'Go back to your hut,' ordered Shaka. 'I have no more to say to you.'

Ntombazi was surprised at this, although she thought that perhaps she had frightened him with her talk of the hyena.

'Is that all?' she asked. 'Is there no punishment?'

'Go back to your hut. A companion awaits you.'

Ntombazi thought Shaka meant that her companion would be her son Zwide, who she did not know was some two hundred miles away. She was taken to the hut by the guards and the door closed behind her leaving little light, except that which penetrated through the grass covering at the top.

She sat in silence.

After a while she became aware of the presence of something alive in the hut. It smelt of an animal and later as her eyes became accustomed to the gloomy light, she saw two glowing eyes staring into hers.

Ntombazi screamed and the guards pulled away some of the grass from the side of her hut, which enabled her to see a lot better. She screamed again, terrified, for sitting there in front of her was a monstrous hyena.

For three days and three nights the beast kept away from Ntombazi, but on the third day, now crazy with hunger, the beast could wait no longer and began to attack her. In mockery Shaka sent her a spear, but this was to be of no avail, for the animal was not to be stopped.

Eventually Shaka gave orders for the hut with its tragic occupants, the half-dead woman and the carrion beast, to be burnt down, so putting an end to the sufferings of the evil woman.

Shaka had insisted from the first time he went to war that war is something total—all must be killed, or escape. He looked upon an enemy as people who must be killed. To him there was no taking of prisoners, for, unlike Dingiswayo, he believed that there could be no second chance for any enemy in case the enemy should win next time.

His belief was now much strengthened since the killing of Dingiswayo, who had deserved to be treated by Zwide as a more worthy enemy whose life should be spared, for Dingiswayo had saved the life of Zwide on several occasions.

Shaka had intended to kill Zwide and his mother for what he believed to be grievous sins against his friend, but he had to be content with his cruel treatment of Ntombazi, knowing that her son had escaped. But Shaka also knew that Zwide would never return, for his people had either fled or had been killed and all their huts had been burned. This to Shaka was total war, which he would always carry out without any fear whatever.

Those who were loyal to him were given everything in his power to give—whether it was feasts, marriage dowries (*lobola*), cattle or land—and to those who were close to him, nothing was too much for him to give. But for his enemies there was no mercy.

When the feasting and the pleasure and the hunting to celebrate the victory over the Ndwandwe were over, Shaka's mind went back to war and the expanding of his country and his people.

He had long looked to the land of the Tembu and now decided he must take it; and so he sent an insulting message to Ngoza, chief of the tribe and overlord of a dozen others, hoping to start a war. And a war did start, as he hoped, for Ngoza was angry and returned the message, warning Shaka to sharpen his spears.

Not needing to be told to make his men ready for war, Shaka moved at once towards the Tembu country. As he went, he split his forces into two parts; one to take on the main weight of the Tembu army, and the other to raid the kraals, driving away the cattle and killing or capturing the Tembu women and children.

For a long time the outcome of the battle was in the balance, but the Tembu men became so alarmed and infuriated when they saw what was happening to their women and children that they were blinded with madness. Then the strict discipline of the Zulu regiments prevailed, and they chased the Tembu from their own territory. Once more Shaka's empire was enlarged.

Now, Shaka decided to spend some time at home, building and re-building his kingdom, while he sent two of his best lieutenants to bring in cattle and any other loot they could acquire, and to bring in any stray human beings who wanted a home, for Shaka needed them for his armies, to die for him in battle.

While on such an expedition, one of these lieutenants, Mzilikazi, deserted Shaka, and went north. He travelled a thousand miles, and there founded the tribe of the Matabele. At first Shaka was angry and sent troops to capture the deserters, but although many of them were killed, Mzilikazi escaped. Later he forgave Mzilikazi, who had named his capital after Shaka's kraal. The Bulawayo of the Matabele eventually gave its name to the modern city of that name in Rhodesia.

Then followed a long period of quiet, during which Shaka began to make sure of those territories he had won. He perfected his legal system which gave him the power of life and death in whatever cruel form he wished, and appeared to enjoy sitting in judgement on his subjects.

He would make up his mind on the instant as to what punishment should be given.

'Twist their necks!' he would say, and everyone knew

well that it would happen that way. There would be no pardon.

During this period, Shaka was visited by English settlers with whom he developed the best of relationships. They traded with him, and they gave him many gifts which he accepted, giving others in return.

Although a tyrant who would not hesitate to sentence a man to death, Shaka admired courage and most of all he admired the English for their bravery in sailing the oceans. This prompted him one day to say that while the Zulu was only afraid of that which he could not see, the English appeared not even to be afraid of that. Coming from such a giant in bravery, that was praise indeed.

Inactivity worried Shaka more than anything else. Often he would organise the biggest hunting expeditions ever seen, but even these did not call for great feats of endurance from him and his men, and one day he decided he would put everybody to the test.

He called all his elders, his advisers, soldiers and officers, and everybody connected with his court and, without having given them any warning, he made them follow him on a great walk round a large part of his country. The pace was so fast that they covered fifty to sixty miles a day and many died on the way, particularly the old men, but Shaka was not in the least concerned. All must finish the course or die.

When he returned to his capital, however, he learned that the sons of Zwide were on the march against the Zulu. They were coming, it was said, with their women, their cattle and all their possessions, to reclaim the land of the Ndwandwe.

Shaka welcomed the news. He assembled his army,

and he even had with him a small number of English settlers from the coast with their primitive firearms, though these weapons were very unreliable. One man named Fynn marched alongside Shaka, and it is through this man that so much is known about the great Zulu king, for Fynn wrote much about his own experiences with Shaka and his warriors.

The battle of Ndololwane soon started and yet another victory was added to that long list of battles already won by Shaka and his warriors. Yet from it one grave tragedy arose. Shaka's very trusted friend, Mgobozi, who had helped Shaka in the early days to train the army, and who had been his most faithful and devoted aid in war and against witchcraft, was killed by the Ndwandwe.

Shaka was very distressed by the news of the death of his friend, and it was a long time before he recovered. Indeed, so angry was he that he killed in the most vicious ways every Ndwandwe man, woman or child to be found, and only a handful with their chiefs escaped, never to trouble Shaka again.

This was to be the last battle in which Shaka took part, and thereafter he went to work almost wholly on civic matters, amongst which was the very important job of moving his capital nearer the coast of Natal and just north of the Umvoti river. He gave the new place the name of Dukuza, which was roughly where Stanga stands today.

Shaka probably did this to be nearer the English, with whom he was intent on establishing the best of relations. He was keen to send an ambassador to King George IV, and appointed several of his tribal elders to accompany one of his white friends to treat with the English. When they reached Cape Town, however, they were met and questioned by government representatives who, not knowing how a Zulu king lived and thought, asked questions which to Shaka's men made no sense whatever.

One of the questions asked by the English was, 'Can Shaka write or make any characters which will show his authority?'

Had Shaka been there he might well have wondered if that was the only way in which one could show authority. Perhaps his answer would have been to throw his spear into the table, or perhaps, indeed, his formidable presence would have made such a question unnecessary.

Chapter 5
A battle against superstition

It was only natural that Shaka, born and raised in the tradition of superstition, should first follow the tribal belief in the power of the witch-doctor, but from the time he began in earnest to build a great people, he took up a fight against the witch-doctors and their magic.

There was a section of the community known as 'witch-finders' whose job was to find the weavers of spells, while using the art of witchcraft themselves. Chief among these creatures was a woman named Nobela, whose influence over the people was almost as great as that of Shaka, for in such matters as witch-finding her authority was supreme and not to be questioned by anyone, not even her chief. This state of affairs led to the carrying out of many tricks and whenever Nobela felt she was not getting what she wanted, or if she felt the least bit jealous of a certain person, she used her supposed powers to 'smell out' her enemy as a witch or other evil-doer. Often she said that such a person was the innocent victim of an evil spirit dwelling in a body which might not be aware of its existence.

Shaka did not believe in such superstition, and he felt he must soon face up to the problem as otherwise his own authority would be challenged. With a people so devoted to belief in witchcraft, he might well find himself in trouble and even become dominated by people like Nobela.

One day he returned from a campaign of conquest to find his kraal in uproar—it was said that crows had perched on his fence speaking in the Zulu tongue and that lightning had struck them dead. It was also said that two cows had died at his kraal gate.

Perhaps Shaka started the disturbance himself, for it was not unknown for him to do this when he wanted to expose trouble-makers. However, he called Nobela to enquire into the cause of the trouble.

Nobela's enquiry took the form of a smelling-out ceremony, when all the people of all the kraals in the area were called together and lined up for close inspection by her and her assistants.

The dress of these evil women and their antics in the fiendish dances with which they started the proceedings were enough to frighten the people almost to death. For the person smelt out the immediate penalty was death, not only for the one concerned, but for his whole family, men, women and children. The witch-finders would take great advantage of their position in this respect and arranged for anyone they did not like or trust to be killed. With no appeal possible, their word was law. Their badge of office was a wildebeeste's tail, which they pointed at their victims, who were instantly seized by those attending on the women, known simply as the 'killers'. If the victims could get away before being seized and sought safety at the feet of the chief, then they might escape with their lives, but the action of the killers was always so swift after the smelling-out that it was usually impossible to claim such sanctuary.

No doubt Shaka suspected that each performance was decided before it started and that the killers were

34

in league with the smellers-out. It certainly looked on this occasion as though Shaka had decided to make some investigation of his own.

It was well known that Nobela had a hatred of Shaka's two lieutenants, Mgobozi and Mdlaka, and the proceedings seemed to show that she intended that the time to kill the two men had come. She went through the long and practised routine of looking into the faces of the hundreds of people, making one 'smelling-out' here and another there, but always coming back to stare with evil vengeance into the faces of Mgobozi and Mdlaka who stood a few feet in front of Shaka.

Shaka, unmoved, called Nobela to him and warned her not to start something which she would not be able to finish.

After taking several more victims from the crowd Nobela worked her way back to Mgobozi and Mdlaka closely followed by her assistants and the killers, the number of which had now grown to twelve, which meant that, if both men were to resist, they had to silence six men each. Inevitably Nobela pointed to the two men, who were not so alert as they should have been. It seemed as if the proceedings had stupefied them as well as everybody else. However, when seized by the killers, both men sprang into action and clubbed their would-be assassins to death before their king, to whom they then rushed to claim sanctuary.

Of course, Shaka did not intend to lose these two most valuable of all his men, but he had to see to it that events were properly organised in the traditional way. So he called Nobela and her assistants to him and accused them of some spite against his two warriors.

'You have made two very bad mistakes, I tell you,' said the king, 'and as always happens to people who make mistakes, you must die. Two of you shall die. Which two I care not. You must choose now!'

The women took to the traditional method of casting lots, that of throwing bones on the ground. Whichever person the bones pointed to was guilty.

The two guilty ones picked out by the bones were Nobela and one of her assistants, but they both rushed with the quickness of cats to the feet of Shaka to beg sanctuary.

'There is no sanctuary here,' said Shaka. 'Sanctuary is only for those who are smelt-out. If you will confess that it was witchcraft you were guilty of, I will give you both sanctuary.'

Anything was better than death by the skewers, and both women immediately branded themselves as evil witches and were then allowed to go.

Shaka recognised the benefits of exploiting the traditions of his people—it made them feel secure, and it made them feel that he was a king who could protect them, a king who could show signs of his protection. When his people felt secure Shaka felt secure also. On one occasion, knowing well that he was watching an eclipse of the sun, he took advantage of the situation to gain great prestige and praise from his people by ordering the sun 'to return to its full splendour which could be seen by his people who wanted also to feel its warmth'. He did this just at the precise moment when he knew that the moon's shadow over the sun was about to move. His motive was simple. 'Magic' for the advancement of Shaka was not a bad thing, but 'magic' used against him or his friends was not to be tolerated. And so, before moving to his new capital at Dukuza, Shaka decided to put an end to witch-doctoring and witch-doctors throughout the land. Unknown to anyone except his counsellor, Mbopa, Shaka sprinkled ox blood all around and over his own hut one night and then went back to bed.

Next morning there was great trouble in the kraal and soon the news spread throughout the kingdom that Shaka had been bewitched. He appeared to be boiling with rage and called a meeting of all those people who lived within a day and a night's march from his kraal, together with every witch-doctor and witch-finder in the land.

On the day appointed nearly two hundred witch-doctors came together at Shaka's kraal and some thousands of people waited for the 'smelling-out' ceremony.

'Smell out the people who insulted me, my tribe and my ancestors!' shouted Shaka, 'and when you have found them herd them into an enclosure and we shall kill them!'

Nobela, enemy of Shaka's friends, looked upon this as an opportunity to rid herself of all those whom she hated. First of all she smelt out the one man who was in the plot, Mbopa, who much to Shaka's amusement had to sit throughout the day in the enclosure apparently awaiting death! Then followed Nqoboka, the Sokulu chief, a life-long friend of Shaka, and then, much to the alarm of the whole company, Mgobozi was sent to sit and wait for death.

At the end of the day several hundred people had been sent into the enclosure by the witch-doctors. However, just two witch-doctors had not sent anyone, so he called them forward to account for themselves.

'Why have you not smelt out any of my people?' he enquired.

They were silent for some time until at last one of them said, 'Do you want to hear the truth, O king?'

'The truth! Yes! Yes! The truth!' shouted Shaka.

'It was done by heaven,' replied one of the men fearfully, for the word *heaven* meant Zulu and it meant that only Shaka knew or else Shaka had done it himself.

Whether Shaka had told the men to say this or not, nobody will ever know, but it provided just the answer he wanted.

'Yes! Yes! You have spoken the truth! I did it myself,' shouted Shaka, leaping to his feet. 'I smeared the blood of an ox all over my hut and all over the ground around it. The witch-doctors are all lying. What shall we do with them, my people? What shall we do with them?'

Angrily, the people shouted for the same to happen to the witch-doctors as they would have arranged for their victims.

'The death of the skewers!' thundered the people. 'Give them the death of the skewers!'

And the witch-doctors met the death of the skewers —all except Nobela, who poisoned herself. At a stroke Shaka had stamped out the practice of witchcraft in the land.

Chapter 6
Shaka's downfall

Although Shaka had moved his kraal to the new capital of Dukuza, his mother continued to live in her kraal at Bulawayo some fifty miles away, where she spent much of her time with her grandson, Shaka's only child whose mother was Mbuzikazi, one of his 'sisters' as they were called.

For a long time Shaka was unaware that he had a son, but eventually he learned about it and he decided to visit his mother.

Shaka greeted his mother, who had the child with her.

'It would be better if I killed him now,' he said, 'for I shall never want him and he will not be a chief, for Mbuzikazi is not of royal blood.'

'You shall not kill the child. I want to keep it,' replied Nandi. 'If you still want to kill somebody, it would be better if you took the lives of your half-brothers, Dingane and Mhlangana, for they are dangerous. One day they'll kill you!'

'All right, mother. You shall keep the child, but you must not expect me to kill the children of my father.'

'But you'd kill your own child and think nothing of it,' answered his mother. 'I warn you—beware of your two half-brothers and your counsellor, Mbopa, for he is plotting with them to kill you. I will send this innocent child away, for when they have killed you they will kill him.'

When Shaka had left, the child and his mother

Mbuzikazi were sent by Nandi to live with friends in the land of the Tembe. Heart-broken, Nandi soon fell ill, and when Shaka heard of this he immediately set off to return to her kraal with his white friend Fynn. Together they arrived at Nandi's kraal just before she died.

Fynn records that he thought Nandi had died of dysentery, and tells the story in these words:

'When Shaka heard the news that his mother was dead, he stood for a long time, head bowed, leaning on his shield, seemingly rooted to the spot. Suddenly he broke out into the most frightening yells.

The signal was enough. The chiefs and people to the number of about fifteen thousand commenced the most dismal and horrid noises. The people from the neighbouring kraals, male and female, came pouring in, each body as they came in sight, at a distance of half a mile, joining to swell the terrible cry. Through the whole of the night it continued, none daring to rest or refresh themselves with water; while from time to time, fresh shouts were heard as more regiments approached. The morning dawned without any lessening of the noise and before noon the number had increased to about sixty thousand. The cries became horrid. Hundreds were lying faint through tiredness and want of food, while forty dead oxen lay in a heap as an offering to the father spirits of the tribe.

At noon the whole force formed a circle with Shaka in the centre and sang a war-song. At the close of it, Shaka ordered several men to be executed on the spot; the cries became, if possible more violent than ever. No further orders were needed, but the people started a general massacre. Many of them received the blow of death while giving it to others. Towards afternoon, I thought that the dead amounted to about seven thousand.'

Three days after her death, and amid such terrible scenes, Ndlovukazi, mother of Shaka and the Zulu people, was buried with ten servants whose arms and legs had been broken before they were killed.

Twelve thousand warriors attended the burial and afterwards guarded the grave for a year; during this time they ate fifteen thousand oxen which were taken from all over the country.

After his mother's death, Shaka seemed to go completely mad. He had always paid little attention to human life, but now he killed for no reason at all. He called the Zulu people together again and again just for the purpose of killing. He put to death a whole tribe, who he said had not shown enough respect or sympathy to him in his great and dreadful sorrow; he blamed various groups of people for having brought about Nandi's death and murdered them in large numbers; he ordered a large number of women to be put to death by having burning thatch tied to their backs; and he butchered hundreds of cows in order that their calves should know the sorrow of Shaka in his orphanhood.

Such insane cruelty could have only one result: state affairs were not attended to and the country, without firm leadership, began to suffer. Harvests were not gathered—the land began to be overgrown with weeds and covered in rubbish. Animals were neglected, and valuable calves died from lack of food.

Shaka had till now, been one of the most influential men in the whole of Africa, but his behaviour now not only left his country so much the poorer but started thoughts of rebellion in the minds of his subjects. Such ideas were especially dangerous to Shaka who had many half-brothers jealous of his power. A rumour that Shaka had killed his mother spread all over the country. People began to believe it and at the same time wondered whether he was still sane. Probably his half-brothers were now starting such rumours to help them in their attempts to seize power.

But Shaka ignored the danger and spent more of his time in inactivity at his kraal at Dukuza. The spirit of adventure appeared to have gone from his life. He passed much of the day with the Europeans, King (who had returned with his mission to Cape Town) and Fynn, listening to what they had to say about other parts of the world they had seen. The rest of his days and nights he spent with Pampata, to whom he had now turned for comfort in his feeling of insecurity.

'Your people are in need of you, Shaka,' said Pampata one day. 'Our country is unhappy—our cattle are dying—the life has left our people.'

At last Pampata managed to make an impression on Shaka.

'You are right, Pampata. We have much to give my people. I will go out and make a visit to every part of my kingdom and rouse the warriors, the old men, the women and the children. I will do great things again. Who do you know to be my enemies?'

'Only your brothers Dingane and Mhlangana; all the people of the Zulu know this, my king, except you.'

43

'They are too fat and lazy. They will do me no harm,' replied Shaka. 'If the time came when they attacked me, then I would kill them, but not before.'

But it was to happen the way Nandi and Pampata had warned Shaka. One evening, just as Shaka was preparing to leave on his great visit, the two half-brothers, Dingane and Mhlangana, with the counsellor, Mbopa, went to Shaka's kraal.

Shaka was unarmed, except for the small red-handled spear he carried as his symbol of office. Without warning the three of them sank their spears into him and left him there to die. Shaka crashed to the ground, mortally wounded.

Quickly the assassins left, followed by the whole of the people in Dukuza, who were too frightened to stop. Only Pampata stayed to lie, weeping, across the dead body of her king—her lover—the great Shaka, while a storm raged and washed away the royal blood from both of them.

In the night, attracted by the smell of death, hyenas came prowling by, but Pampata kept them away all night, and in the morning they slunk off.

Seeing all the footprints of the hyena and her own footprints too, Pampata thought up a plan to add some glory to Shaka's death. She covered her own footprints to make it appear that only the hyena had been near, and then away she went in search of help to remove Shaka's body.

The three assassins now returned, thinking the body would have been eaten by the hyena. They were astonished at what they found—Shaka lay untouched! Thus arose the Zulu legend that the hyena will always leave the body of a dead king.

Shaka's half-brothers and Mbopa buried the king in an upright position, dressed in all his royal clothes and with all his weapons, but without ceremony. The one thing they could not find was his badge of office, the little red-handled spear—Pampata had taken it, and they found her with its point in her heart.

Questions

CHAPTER 4

1. What justification did Shaka have for killing his enemies so ruthlessly?
2. What test did Shaka devise for the leaders of the Zulus and what was its outcome?
3. How do we know so much about the history of Shaka?
4. What kind of proof did the British want of Shaka's authority?

CHAPTER 5

1. Why did Shaka wish to destroy witchcraft in his kingdom?
2. How did Shaka destroy Nobela's power? Describe the incident in your own words.
3. How did Shaka impress his people when the sun was eclipsed?
4. How did Shaka destroy the power of the witch-doctors? Describe the incident in your own words.

CHAPTER 6

1. How did Shaka behave when his mother died?
2. Why did his people begin to think of rebellion?
3. Why did Shaka not kill Dingane and Mhlangana? (He gave one reason to his mother before she died and another to Pampata when she tried to stir him to action.)
4. The Zulu legend says that the hyena will always leave the body of a dead king. How did this legend arise?
5. How did Pampata prove her love for Shaka?

What do you think of Shaka? Was he a good chief?
What was admirable in his character? Was he right
always to be so ruthless with his enemies? What were
his weaknesses?